T0062235

I Threw a Star in a Wine Glass

*

Short poems

Fethi Sassi

Mwanaka Media and Publishing Pvt Ltd,
Chitungwiza Zimbabwe

*

Creativity, Wisdom and Beauty

Publisher:

Mmap

Mwanaka Media and Publishing Pvt Ltd

24 Svosve Road, Zengeza 1

Chitungwiza Zimbabwe

mwanaka@yahoo.com

https//mwanakamediaandpublishing.weebly.com

Distributed in and outside N. America by African Books Collective

orders@africanbookscollective.com

www.africanbookscollective.com

ISBN: 978-0-7974-9335-3

EAN: 9780797493353

© Fethi Sassi 2018

All rights reserved.

No part of this book may be reproduced or transmitted in any form or by any means, mechanical or electronic, including photocopying and recording, or be stored in any information storage or retrieval system, without written permission from the publisher

DISCLAIMER

All views expressed in this publication are those of the author and do not necessarily reflect the views of *Mmap*.

Contents Table

Introduction

With love and soft fragrance, works the poet *Fethi Sassi* to realize a dream that was until now breathing in the depth of his personality; that's why he translated these poems into English and to some other languages to throw his love's call to humanity, singing for others a chant never to stop until the last day of the old earth. This careful selection of short poems, *I Threw a Star in a Wine Glass*, already written in Arabic original language, translated into English, with a big tendency in the recurrent theme of love and sensual and erotic desire, can offer you a passport to live for other planets never imagined. Though I am sure how difficult it is to write about love, just because when a poet wants to go this road he has to write a special and original poem because all the themes have been invaded by almost all the poets in history, that's why some poets wrote only a few love poems but others kept sculpting in time until they offered great masterpieces.

Finally; it's a very harsh target to create some new masterpieces with a high authenticity and beauty.

As for the poems in *I Threw a Star in a Wine Glass*, love is beginning to be not only a theme or even poetry, but love is religion and all poems are no more than a prophet who gives the chance for people to go in the same way.

But what is left unsaid after all the parts of the poem stop their simultaneous motion in the reader's depth. Something that is almost without a word to name it grows in that very moment creating a spiritual erotic emotion, an inner desire for love that turns in its sensuality into a prayer in silence.

We are not to forget that our poet is a faithful reader of poetry, in this world he experienced a high degree of a spiritual love and erotic sense, as he created or recreated the wonderful desire in memory to shine as an eternal immanent present but magically embodied in a certain transcendent manner, where the sacred and the profane embrace each other and unify. There's only one space to make such "contradictions" brace coherently enlightening the obscure zones in human soul: the poem.

Here is a collection of poems, selected and translated by the poet himself, and presented as a blue gate of Eden. Together, these poems form a book that throws love in a cup of wine, but also a deep doorway to a new aesthetic experience. Thanks to the poet's longing for a great love and sensual poem, this creative translation incarnated so much of the poems' spirit, in the English language, which is a new vision for the eternal deep feelings.

Preface

Is there enough room on this earth for my dreams?

Poems

Rain

If I were rain,
I would drench all languages.

Fever

How could this simple kiss do to my body
all this fever?

Clouds

Indeed…
Love is what the clouds have written.

Cigarettes

On your body,
I try to collect my cigarettes.
Perhaps, I discover an idea for the ash.

A rain drop

You suddenly fall from the sky,
as a raindrop,
I wonder from which cloud you came.

Inside a Cloud

My mistress,
If we were to live together inside a cloud,
we would rain a fall of lust.

Besieged

The rose that grow on your cheeks,
Besieged the poem of all the poets.

Papers of whiteness

At night,
whenever I stumbled upon a poem,
I find it lonesome, flirting with papers of
whiteness,
on the edge of the night.

Happiness

On the banks of my dreams, I drink my
evening coffee.
Happy with my obsessions,
Jotting my coming losses.

Excitation

My beloved;
wear the moon a dress for our wedding.
I will gift you a dream as exciting as a star,
Wet as a cloud.

The presence of the devil

In the presence of the devil
I dipped in you my most beautiful sins.
Will the poets forgive my deeds?

Rain child

And whenever I chose a cloud in my cup;
flowed languages out of me,
and I dropped down like a rain child.

The mud

O… Cloud, what happened to you.
That made you hide in my blood;
and raise the whims of mud?

This morning

The sun woke up and wiped its lids,
and threw on the night,
to give warmth to the words.

This is a kiss

And when I kissed her,
I sweep the world in a poem.

.

The prisoner

In fear; I ask myself:
Is that anger the mole trapped between her
eyebrows.

Dictionary for my poems

And from your face,
I made up a dictionary for all my poems.

The black man

On her cheeks slowly swings the night,
as a black magician,
that draws a blond star in the sky.

9

We will never meet

We don't meet,
however,
nostalgia used to bring us together.

Verbalizing

How come you chatter,
and you are a women who refuse verbalizing?

Mail

The sea got angry with me;
so it sent me the mail of the wind.

Defeats

My beautiful lady,
rain over me , for I am the tired soil,
lusting for my defeats.

Wines

By god!
How I found you on the step of the poem,
drunken from the wines of the context!!

Threads

My warm woman,
Give me a thread of your femininity,
So that I see my defeats in the gardens of your
body.

A question

Why do words fail me when I say;
I love you??
And the whiteness takes fire.

Departure

How do you suddenly leave
Letting my fingertips quivering
in your absence?

Every moment

The whiteness asks me every moment
Who is this woman,
Whom you write about all these things?

From your eyes

The comers, the passers and the returnees,
from your eyes,
they forget their words on the road.

"Neruda"

A man who clutters my papers every night,
Named (Neruda),
Humors me when I flirt with the narcissism of
the place,
and hallucinates a poem for the lust of the wait
.

Spaces

How much lust do I need,
So that I cover all the space on your body?

Last dance

There,
warmer than poetry,
I meet with (Zorba) to have the last dance
together,
in the poets bar.

In the balcony

What happened to my beloved?
She no longer drinks her coffee on the balcony,
of my sorrows.

The writing

I write your name a thousand times,
and do it all over again,
and I might learn writing.

A thousand palm trees

On your face,
full of love, I will plant a thousand palm trees,
where all lovers shall meet.

Lonely

Lonely;
I drink a coffee on the porch,
and laugh like an old tree in a garden,
Lonely;
I forgot a hanging look on the moon's
forehead.

Harassment

Close to you,
I get this feeling that I'm in a garden,
And that all the roses are harassing me.

Only for absence

Usually,
it happens that during the absence,
I don't forget you.

A butterfly

My heart is a butterfly;
spinning your lips with sun,
and studding my body with your kisses.

A crack

You left.
And my dreams cracked.

A flying butterfly

Each time you kissed me,
I became a butterfly.

Jealousy

The moon has closed its eyes,
When the star has been painting its nails with
black paint.

Children of the star

O…sons of the drunken star,
come out and play in the gardens of dawn.

Rains of kisses

When we used to sit under the rains of kisses,
I used to get wet with you all alone.

Braids

I embroidered your lips with threads of light.
That were wandering on your crazy braids.

9

Confession

Whenever I poured my blood in a poem,
I ripped my memory.

The lovers

I'm no priest and I never preached the poets
(Sura).
My poetry is a temple for lovers;
and a clinic for women.
I establish a religion for love, and send my
prophets.

Rains

The drizzling rain is sad this morning,
for my cloud didn't rain on your eyebrows.

A drowning state

Your scent keeps me company every night.
And clouds drown in my blood.

A look

Here everything is over,
nothing has remained other than
that watering look in her eyes.

Incense

I will put a little incense;
On your lips
So that lovers seep into my blood.

The scent of clouds

At sunset,
the poem lies on the sand,
under the scent of the cloud, and keeps
singing.

After you

And after you;
no perfume has ever smelled nice,
and Jasmine lost its charm.

A story

Her eyes tell the story of light;
that hung to the sun's fingertips,
swimming in the cloud's realm.

Tapsters

At the hearing of the twilight;
the goddess used to sit with her tapsters,
drinking destinies with the sun's wine,
and the moon's saliva.

A rain of words

When I start writing, snarls the sky,
in my hand,
and rains words.

Loss

Your face had become my compass,
for when I get lost between the shadows.

The spikes

As usual,
I threw ears of wheat on my way;
and fly with pigeons every morning.

Awaiting

In the hospital of letters,
I visit languages.
And await the birth of the poem.

To my mother

O mother;
Take me to my sad coffee,
To the smell of coffee in your eyes.
Take me
to a woman who flirts the goddess, and that
the prophets abandon.

The fugitive

I glimpsed at the end of the night,
a star running away from the moon's looks
in the sky.

A painter's thought

Whenever I drew you,
I made your face a sun, and your dreams stars,
And then got lost, solitary in the clouds.

Stories

With every rain drop,
falls a story of a cloud.

Blame

A song blaming a bird,
and says to it:
why did you leave me all alone among the
words?

The dust of memories

I look for you;
and you are buried among the dust of
memories,
and the salts of clouds.

The sidewalk

Only the sidewalk; knows
the echo of my footsteps,
when I used to wait for you.

Weeping

The doves
speaks to me about your absence,
and weeps.

Didn't happen

I still prepare a beautiful morning for her.
And hang a drop of water to a dream;
that didn't happen yet.

6

Give me

This night is rainy in my language,
so give me your hands to wipe the eye clouds.

Fires

The wind is in delirium as a magician's shiver,
Flirting, a fairy that gives the fire the taste of
oysters.

The defeat

This whiteness no longer beats me,
one poem is enough,
for my rest.

A glass of wine

I threw a star in a glass of wine,
and got drunk.

A flirt

While the winds where embroidered with words and letters.
I flirted with its little daughter.

The poem of winter

O… sun, lend me your fingers,
to give warmth to the poem of winter.

My small basket

At dawn,
I carry my small basket,
and fill my palm with the sighs of the flute.

The fingerprint of my thumb

I chant an overflowing star in the fingerprint
of my thumb,
while I sign her name in the sky.

Greetings

Every morning your eyes have a balcony,
that grows greetings of the night,
in a pot of lust.

So

So I still light all my poems,
in your eyes.

A devil

I used to ask myself:
Why has the devil driven me away from your
eyes?

To *the lunatic*

O you crazy women,
You will not fit anywhere but in my poems.

Hope

Don't be saddened.
These clouds shall pass,
and will stay our love.

A meeting

In the absence of the ink,
we met.
The place was devoid of everything except of
her laugh.

I need you

Don't leave my smile just yet,
I need you to hide the morning in another
cloud.

One woman

There;
is only one woman that inhabits this night,
covered with my body, when I burn in my
awe.

Fear

When you kiss the rose,
I fear that you get wounded by the gasp.

Drowning

How I love this water in your eyes!
There is no need to drown.

Only the cloud

Before the spray took its life, only the cloud
hears me,
On the tables of the rain.

.

A star kiss

It is useless to be kissed by a star,
and this night is watching me.

For what

Under my pillow,
I hear the whispering of the light,
for what purpose is the night bathing in my
room.

A poem

Glowing as a scream,
that is the way I look when I am writing a
poem.

Tell every cloud

Winds! Tell every cloud,
to hold an umbrella so that the light stays dry
.

Fall

Take me, you star,
so that I do not fall apart like dust.

A dream

And I dream of a star in my coat,
and winds pushing me towards the sky.

An invitation

Last night, I got invited by a star.
To light up all this sky together.

A balcony

From a balcony hanging in my heart,
I looked upon the star that bathed in the
moon's saliva.

Seduction

What seduces me the most is the kiss of twilight,
upon the sunset's forehead.

A smart cloud

A smart cloud asks me:
How I manage to sleep inside the poem,
without being wet by visions!

A phobia

O... gorgeous lady,
drink me,
to set me free of drowning phobia.

Eye glasses

Your poem had to wear glasses,
to be able to see my face stuck in the speech.

In the marble

O… heart!
Please do not be quiet,
until I kiss my cloud in the marble.

A bouquet of clouds

The night passes by as a stranger,
to put into your coat a bouquet of clouds.

Embrace

A moment of embrace;
I wanted to remember her hands,
when I was at the last line naming her night.

Printed in the United States
By Bookmasters